W9-BIY-998

Survival
French

Survival
French

by Diethard Lübke
illustrated by Theo Scherling

LANGENSCHEIDT PUBLISHERS
New York, Berlin, Munich, Vienna, Zurich

Publisher:	Langenscheidt Publishers, Inc.
Managing Editor:	Jessie G. McGuire
U.S. Editorial Direction:	Anne & Jean Wadier
U.S. Adaptation:	Anne & Jean Wadier
Cover Design:	Vera Benson
Production:	Ripinsky & Company
Letters:	We welcome your comments and suggestions.

Our address: Langenscheidt Publishers, Inc.
46-35 54th Road
Maspeth, NY 11378

Important Reader Information

We have not burdened you with special grammatical rules. Phonetic transcriptions have been simplified as much as possible and are found in the grey boxes next to the English/French word list in each chapter.

This will also help you to fill in the cartoon balloons with French phrases. Each blank line stands for one letter. For an example, refer to page 10.

To make things easier for you, English sentence structure has been adjusted to the French phrases. Therefore, English sentences may sound somewhat clumsy at times.

Throughout the book, only the latest facts are given, as of 1990. They were carefully checked by the author and the publisher. However, we are not responsible for any changes that may have occured.

© 1991 by Langenscheidt Publishers, Inc., Maspeth, NY 11378
All rights reserved under international and Pan American copyright conventions.

Translated, adapted and revised from *Französisch—Jetzt in Comics*, © 1988 by Humboldt-Taschenbuchverlag Jacobi KG, München.

Manufactured in the United States of America

ISBN: 0-88729-257-7

Contents

Bonjour, mesdames et messieurs,

We are pleased that you want to start learning French and intend to travel to France. Many tourists visit France every year because they love **la cuisine, le soleil, les plages** and much more.

Knowing a little French will help you understand and be understood in typical situations - and your attempts to speak French will be appreciated by everyone you encounter.

This entertaining and informative approach to the language does not require you to "cram" vocabulary and "slave over" grammar, as in school. It does not prepare you for a test, but rather is simply meant to afford you greater pleasure on your vacation, without requiring much effort. Make yourself comfortable, pick up a pencil. You will see that learning French can be very enjoyable.

So you can get right into the swing of things, we have prepared cartoon balloons for you to fill in. Each blank stands for one letter.

And now we will introduce a few important words. The pronunciation is in square brackets:

Bonjour	[bôNzhoor]	*Hello*
Ça va?	[sä vä]	*How are you?*
Au revoir	[ō revô•är]	*Good bye*
Oui	[oo•ē]	*Yes*
Non	[nôN]	*No*
Merci	[mersē]	*Thank you*

vôl säN seNk	le vol 105	flight 105
dōō pär	d'où part . . . ?	where does . . . leave?
pôrt (däNbärkmäN)	la porte (d'embarquement)	gate
nēmärō dā	numéro deux	number 2
zhə vōōdrā	Je voudrais	I would like
äNrezhēstrā	enregistrer	to check (luggage)
mā bägäzh	mes bagages	my luggage
kärt	la carte	boarding pass
däNbärkmäN	d'embarquement	
vôt (ər)	votre	your
trā byeN	très bien,	very well,
byeN	bien	O.K., fine
məsyā	monsieur, M.	sir, Mr.
bôN vô•äyäzh	Bon voyage!	Have a good trip!
sēl vōō plā	s'il vous plaît	please
mersē	merci	thank you

Gender

In French, nouns are masculine (**le** lit, **le** jour) or feminine (**la** chambre).

Le/Un, La/Une

The definite article is **le/la;** the indefinite article is **un/une.** Example: **le** jus/**un** jus; **la** chambre/**une** chambre.

Plural

The ending **-s** indicates the plural.

9

1 Airport

NOTE: Answers for the dialogues in each chapter can be found starting on page 78.

11

loo•ä ën vô•ätēr	**louer une voiture**	*to rent a car*
läzhäNs de lôkäsyôN	**l'agence de location**	*car rental agency*
lôtōrōot	**l'autoroute**	*highway*
sēpär	**le super**	*super (gas)*
lôrdēnär	**l'ordinaire**	*regular (gas)*
pleN	**le plein**	*full tank*
tēkä	**le ticket**	*ticket*
fräN	**le franc**	*franc*
träNt fräN	**trente francs**	*30 francs*
oo	**ou**	*or*
oo•e	**oui**	*yes*

Pronunciation

In French, the nasals are the typical sound. **An, en, in, on, un** . . . are pronounced through the nose. As in **M**o**n**tmartre [môN-märt(ər)], Verd**un** [värdeN]. [zh] is pronounced like **G**énie, **J**alousie, **R**age.

Routes départementales, nationales et autoroutes

In France, to drive from one city to another, you may well have a choice between several itineraries. The road network is indeed extensive: secondary roads (**routes départementales**) are usually picturesque and may be winding; primary roads (**routes nationales**) are more busy and direct, although they pass through the town centers. If you plan to cover a lot of the country though, your best option is the highway (**autoroute**). Check the toll first and watch your speed.

Speed Limits

Autoroutes (highways): 130 km/h. **Routes nationales** (primary roads), **routes départementales** (secondary roads): 90 km/h, in towns: 50-60 km/h.

If a previous road sign is repeated (as a reminder), it also contains the symbol **Rappel**.

2 Car

Organize a trip from *Paris* to the *Côte d'Azur*. You may wish to consult a road map or atlas.

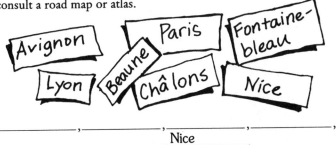

_____, _____, _____, _____,
_____, _____ Nice _____.

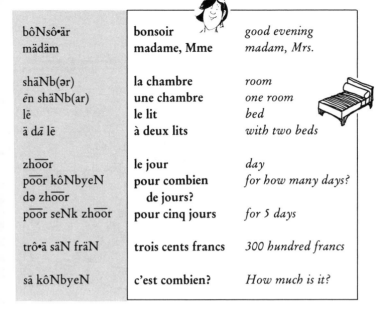

bôNsô•är	**bonsoir**	*good evening*
mädäm	**madame, Mme**	*madam, Mrs.*
shäNb(ər)	**la chambre**	*room*
ēn shäNb(ar)	**une chambre**	*one room*
lē	**le lit**	*bed*
ä dä lē	**à deux lits**	*with two beds*
zhoor	**le jour**	*day*
poor kôNbyeN də zhoor	**pour combien de jours?**	*for how many days?*
poor seNk zhoor	**pour cinq jours**	*for 5 days*
trô•ä säN fräN	**trois cents francs**	*300 hundred francs*
sä kôNbyeN	**c'est combien?**	*How much is it?*

Guide Michelin

When traveling in France, the latest edition of this book is highly recommended. It contains listings of many hotels and restaurants as well as maps of all large cities.

---

* The balloons at the beginning of each lesson are illustrations only and do not require you to translate them.

3 Hotel

____ _____ __ _____?
For how many days?

____ ____ _____.
For five days.

_'___ _____, __ _____?
How much is the room?

_____ ____ _____.
300 hundred francs.

____ _____.
Very well.

→
3 Yes
5 Good evening
6 Room
7 Bed
8 Sir

↓ 1 Very well, O.K.
2 Day
4 How much

19

bôNzhoor	**bonjour**	*good morning*
pətē dāzhānā	**le petit déjeuner**	*breakfast*
käfā	**le café**	*coffee*
käfā ō lā	**le café au lait**	*coffee with milk*
tā	**le thé**	*tea*
eN zhē dôräNzh	**un jus d'orange**	*an orange juice*
krô•äsäN	**le croissant**	*croissant*
kôNfétēr	**la confiture**	*jam*
bār	**le beurre**	*butter*
voo dāzērā	**vous désirez?**	*What would you like?*
vôä•lä	**voilà**	*here it is*
oo	**où**	*where*
sā too	**c'est où?**	*where is it?*
ä drôät	**à droite**	*to/on the right*
ä gōsh	**à gauche**	*to/on the left*
ā	**et**	*and*

Tu/Vous

Vous is used as the polite form of address while **tu** applies to less formal relationships between friends and relatives. Young people tend to use **tu** all the time between themselves. When in doubt, play it safe and **vouvoyer** (use **vous**).

Liaisons

A lot of words are linked together in French speech. You will soon know when to do this (**faire la liaison**).
Ex.: **les petits enfants** [läpətēzäNfäN]

4 Breakfast

Petit déjeuner 4

_____ __ ____,
Here is the coffee,

___ _____,
the croissants,

__ _____
the jam

__ __ _____.
and the butter.

____ _____ __ __ _'_____?
Do you want orange juice?

___!
Yes!

→
3 Juice
4 Coffee

↓
1 Hello
2 Butter

23

In the morning,
a visit to the Louvre.
In the afternoon . . .

pläN	**le plan**	*map, plan*
pläN də pärē	**le plan de Paris**	*map of Paris*
mātrō	**le métro**	*subway*
stätsyôN də mātrō	**la station de métro**	*subway station*
mātrō vä ä	**le métro va à ...**	*the subway goes to ...*
zhə nə sā pä	**je ne sais pas**	*I don't know*
pärdôN	**pardon**	*excuse me*
mersē bōkoo	**merci beaucoup**	*thank you very much*
too drô•ä	**tout droit**	*straight ahead*
loov(ər)	**le Louvre**	*the Louvre*
bēyā	**le billet**	*ticket*
eN bēyā	**un billet**	*a ticket*

Negation

In French, **Not** is expressed with the two words: **ne ... pas**. In some shortened sentences however, you'll hear the second part only: **j'sais pas**.

Métro

In Paris there are 16 subway lines and 273 stations. In order to find your way around the stations, just remember the last stop of the Metro-Line.

SORTIE = exit, **CORRESPONDANCE** = connection

Museums

The National Museums are generally closed on Tuesdays. Since the opening times of other museums may be different, check them beforehand. Two museums in Paris are well worth the visit: the **Musée d'Orsay** and the **Centre Pompidou**.

5 Museum

5 Museum

Musée 5

A ticket, please.

→
3 Many, a lot
5 Subway
7 Yes
10 Map
11 Thank you
12 Station

↓ 1 Louvre
2 Excuse me
4 Where
6 Ticket
8 Paris
9 Museum

6 Coffee with milk
Café au lait

After three hours in the museum . . .*

Time to take a coffee break!

OLYMPIA

PARIS

shō	chaud	warm, hot
ēl fā shō	il fait chaud	it's hot
āmārēkeN	Américain	American (male)
āmārēken	Américaine	American (female)
lāzātäzēnē	les États-Unis	the United States
fräNs	la France	France
də nōō yôrk	de New York	from New York
zhə sē•ē	je suis	I am
vōōz āt	vous êtes	You are
zhām	j'aime	I love
lāzātäzēnē sôN bō	les Etats-Unis sont beaux	The United States is beautiful
ôsē	aussi	also
sēgäret	la cigarette	cigarette

Cigarettes

At the **Bureau de Tabac,** you can buy cigarettes, cigars and tobacco. It is often part of the café itself and many small articles are also sold there: stamps, pens, newspapers, etc. Look for this sign.

---

* "Olympia" is a famous painting by Edouard Manet (1863).

6 Coffee with milk

lēnet də sôlā•ē	**lunettes de soleil**	*sunglasses*
ā ävek səlä	**et avec cela?**	*something else?*
tōō	**tout**	*all, everything*
sā tōō	**c'est tout**	*that's all*
bēro də	**le bureau de**	*exchange office*
shäNzh	change	
bäNk	**la banque**	*bank*
shäNzhā	**changer**	*to exchange, change*
zhe vä	**je veux**	*I want to exchange*
shäNzhā.	changer	
dôlär	**les dollars**	*American dollars*
āmärēkeN	américains	
mēl	**mille**	*one thousand*
säN	**cent,**	*one hundred,*
dā säN	deux cents	*two hundred*
päspôr	**le passeport**	*passport*
vôt (ər) päspôr	**votre passeport**	*your passport*
läbä	**là-bas**	*over there*
ô revô•är	**au revoir**	*good bye*

Banks

Open 8:00 A.M. to 4:00 P.M., Monday through Friday and Saturday from 8:00 A.M. to 12:00 P.M., unless otherwise specified. Check local branches.

Poste et Caisse d'Epargne

In France, you can also do banking at the post office (**CCP—Compte Chèques Postaux**).

Lunettes de soleil

This word is always used in the plural.

35

7 Exchange

Change 7

— ——— ———?
Something else?

————, '——— ————.
Thank you, that's all.

— ——— ——
Where is the
————— —— ——————?
exchange office?

— —————— —— ——————?
The exchange office?
— ———————- —————————
The "Société-Générale"
——— —— - ———.
is over there.

7 Exchange

BANQUE

Caisse 1

————————, ————————.
Hello, sir.
—— ———— ————————
I want to exchange
———— ————
200
————————.
dollars.

———— ————————, —' —— ———— ————.
Your passport, please.
———— ———— ————————.
Here is 1,000 francs.

_____, _____. __ _____.
Thank you, sir. Good bye.

And now let's buy me
a new handbag: un sac.

4 → All
5 Passport
7 Sir
8 There
9 Thank you
10 One thousand
11 (Sun)glasses
12 Franc

↓ 1 Exchange
2 Office
3 One hundred
6 Sun

kärt pôstäl	**la carte postale**	*postcard*
sä kärt pôstäl	**ces cartes postales**	*these postcards*
teNb(ər)	**le timbre**	*stamp*
läNvelôp	**l'enveloppe**	*envelope*
vōō ävä	**vous avez**	*Do you have*
dā teNb(ər)	**des timbres?**	*any stamps?*
pōōr lä fräNs	**pour la France?**	*for France?*
pôst	**la poste**	*post office*
d*a* fräN	**deux francs**	*two francs*

Mailboxes

Mailboxes are painted yellow. In major cities check the location of the sorting office (**centre de tri**) or certain mail boxes—where mail is collected late. Also, stamps can be purchased at the tobacconist's (**tabac**).

P. et T.

This is the abbreviation for **Postes et Télécommunications**. The acronym P.T.T. (Poste, Télégraphe, Téléphone) is also found.

8 Postcards

How much is

a postcard

for the United States?

2 francs 40.

5 stamps,

please.

Timbres

→
4 Card

↓ 1 Franc
2 Stamp
3 Post office

43

pläzh	la plage	beach
pādälo	le pédalo	paddle boat
päräsol	le parasol	beach umbrella
lē•ēl sôlar	l'huile solaire	suntan oil
zhə vo͞odrā	je voudrais	I would like
ēn gläs	une glace	an ice cream
vänē'ē	vanille	vanilla
shôkôlä	chocolat	chocolate
fräz	fraise	strawberry
lār	l'heure	hour, time
pär ār	par heure	per hour
veN fräN	vingt francs	20 francs
shār	cher	expensive

Beaches

Tourists do not have to pay to go to the beach in France (exception: some beaches on the Côte d'Azur).

Among the many nice beaches: **Côte d'Azur** (St.-Tropez, Cannes, Nice); **Côte Atlantique** (Les-Sables-d'Olonne, Ile d'Oléron, Arcachon, Biarritz); **Bretagne** (La Baule, Quiberon); **Normandie** (Dieppe, Deauville) . . .

9 At the Beach

9 At the beach

3

5 Expensive

7

8 Vanilla

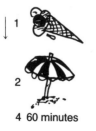

1

2

4 60 minutes

6 Well, O.K., fine

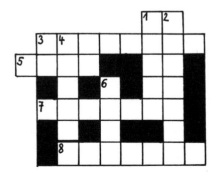

frē•ē	**les fruits**	*fruit*
ēn ôräNzh	**une orange**	*an orange*
bänän	**la banane**	*banana*
bänän	**les bananes**	*bananas*
bänän	**les bananes**	*the bananas*
sôNtekseläNt	**sont excellentes**	*are excellent*
tômät	**la tomate**	*tomato*
säläd də	**la salade de**	*tomato salad*
tômät	**tomates**	
la'ē	**l'ail**	*garlic*
eN kēlo də	**un kilo de**	*a kilo of*
däN	**dans**	*in*
regärdā	**regardez . . .**	*look . . .*
nôN	**non**	*no*
sē	**si**	*yes*

Markets

Do not miss the picturesque marketplaces in major cities and most
small French towns. Local farmers sell their fruit and vegetables
there. There are also other various stands (flowers, clothes . . .).
Paris has separate flower and bird markets, to name but two.

10 Fruit

_____ _____,
What would you like,
_____?
madam?

_____ _____.
5 oranges.

__ ____ ____?
Something else?

_ ____ __ _____,
A kilo of tomatoes
_, __ ____ _____.
please.

___ _____
The bananas
____ _____.
are excellent.

___, _____.
No, thank you.

52

_____ _'___.
Look at the garlic.

___, ___!
No, no!

__!
Yes!
_'___ ___ ____ ___
Garlic is very good

____ __ _____ __ _____.
in tomato salad.

1

2 Salad

3

4

älō	**allô**	*hello*
rāzervā	**réserver**	*to reserve*
zhə vā rāzervā	**je veux réserver**	*I want to reserve*
ēn täb'əl	**une table**	*a table*
persôn	**la personne**	*person*
noN	**le nom**	*name*
vôt(ər) noN	**votre nom**	*your name*
käN	**quand**	*when*
sô•är	**le soir**	*evening*
dəmeN	**demain**	*tomorrow*
spektäkəl	**le spectacle**	*show*
dēnā	**le dîner**	*dinner*

Calling home

Telephones can be found in post offices, cafés and train stations. Also, public telephone booths are usually easy to find. Use 1, 2, 5 and 10 franc coins, telephone tokens (**jetons**) or phone cards. There is a surcharge when calling from hotels or cafés, so check beforehand. Call international information (**les renseignements internationaux**) if no phone book is handy. For the international operator, dial: 19.33.11. For direct international calls, dial: 19 + country code + telephone number.

Cabarets

France has the most famous show theaters in the world: **LE MOULIN ROUGE** (Place Blanche), **LE LIDO** (116 bis, Champs-Elysées), **LE CRAZY HORSE** (12, Avenue George V) and many more.

You need to reserve a table in advance. Admission for dinner, dancing and the show is over 500 francs.

11 Reservations

____.
Hello.

__ ____ _____
I would like to reserve

___ _____
a table

____ ____ _____
for two people

____ _____ ____.
for tomorrow evening.

____. _____ ___,
Very well. Your name,
_,__ ____ _____.
please.

___ ___
My name

___ _____.
is Smith.

12 At the restaurant
Au restaurant

restôräN	le restaurant	*restaurant*
vē•äNd	la viande	*meat*
pô•äsôN	le poisson	*fish*
poolā	le poulet	*chicken*
poolā rôtē	le poulet rôti	*roast chicken*
lômlet	l'omelette	*omelette*
soop	la soupe	*soup*
soop ä lônyôN	la soupe à l'oignon	*onion soup*
pôtäzh	le potage	*soup (thick)*
pôtäzh älätômät	le potage à la tomate	*tomato soup*
läpätē	l'appétit	*appetite*
voozävä termēnä	Vous avez terminé?	*Are you finished?*
voozävä	vous avez	*you have*
lädēsyôN	l'addition	*check*

Restaurants

France is the land of food and wine: there are hundreds and thousands of restaurants to fit everyone's taste and budget. To avoid any unpleasant surprises you might want to purchase a guide; in any case, check the menu (posted at the entrance of most restaurants). Call to find out if reservations are needed.

Mealtimes

Lunch is served between noon and 2 P.M. and dinner after 7 P.M. Some places even start serving as late as 9 P.M.

Habits are still different between Paris and the major cities and the provinces. In Paris, many people just have a quick snack in a café or cafeteria while the two-hour lunch break is still enjoyed in the provinces.

Bread

Crusty French bread is served throughout meals at no charge. You will still even find restaurants where wine and coffee are included in the cost of the meal (country restaurants, "Routiers", etc.).

[Ordering wine, see page 68/69].

12 At the restaurant

____ _____?
What would you like?
_____, _____,
Meat, fish,
_____ ____, _____?
roast chicken, omelette?

____ _____ _____,
Two roast chickens,
_ __ ____ _____.
please.

12 At the restaurant

___ _____?
Soup?
___ _____ _ _'_____?
Onion soup?
__ _____ _ __ _____?
Tomato soup?

____ _____
Two onion
_ _'_____.
soups.   ___.
            Yes.

_'___
Will that be
____?
all?

→
3 Soup
4 Omelette
6 Check
8 Roast
10 Meat

↓ 1 Chicken
2 Appetite

5

7

9

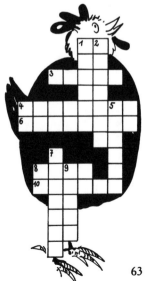

käfä kräm	**le café crème**	*coffee with cream*
kônyäk	**le cognac**	*brandy*
byär	**la bière**	*beer*
veN	**le vin**	*wine*
veN bläN	**le vin blanc**	*white wine*
veN roozh	**le vin rouge**	*red wine*
fräNsä	**français**	*French*

Jean Racey

Produce of France

Beaujolais Villages Primeur

APPELLATION BEAUJOLAIS-VILLAGES CONTROLÉE

Le vin est la plus saine et la plus hygiénique des boissons . . .
PASTEUR

70 cl

Caves du Château de Chénas

IMP CLOS DU MOULIN · 01140 THOISSEY

Mis en bouteille par Jean RACEY à Arnas 69400

dans la région de pro ~tion

French wine
See page 68/69.

13 Drinks

_____, ____ _____?
Hello, what would you like?

__ ____ _____.
A coffee with cream.

__ _____.
A brandy.

__ ___ _ _____,
An orange juice.

Wine with Meals

Many French people have a passion for wine. Wine lovers will go out of their way to carefully match the wine with a meal by selecting a bottle according to the estate (**domaine, château** . . .), vintage and growth (**cru**).

Best wine regions:

	Serving temperature		
	Red:	White:	
	C° / F°	C° / F°	Can be Kept:
BOURGOGNE	15° / 59°	14° / 57°	5–10 years
BORDEAUX*	18° / 64°	8° / 46°	5–15 years
BEAUJOLAIS	12° / 54°		1– 2 years

CHAMPAGNE
Paris
ALSACE
LOIRE
JURA
BOURGOGNE
Cognac
Beaujolais
MEDOC
CÔTES DU RHÔNE
BORDEAUX
LANGUEDOC
PROVENCE
ROUSSILLON

VINS FRANÇAIS

CORSE

Good wine regions:

	Serving temperature		
	Red:	White:	
	C° / F°	C° / F°	Can be kept:
ALSACE		8° / 46°	2-5 years
CÔTES DU RHÔNE	15° / 59°	8° / 46°	2–3 years
PROVENCE	15° / 59°	8° / 46°	1–4 years
LOIRE	15° / 59°	10° / 50°	1–3 years

* MÉDOC, HAUT MÉDOC, GRAVES, MARGAUX . . .

What to drink when you eat . . .

Fish (grilled, boiled, smoked)	Dry white wine **Vin blanc sec**
Oysters, Mussels, Lobster	
Egg dishes	
Hot cheese preparations, Fondue, Quiche	
Poultry, Rabbit, Pork (boiled)	Red or white wine **Vin rouge ou vin blanc** (i.e. Bourgogne, Chardonnay)
Vegetables, Poultry, Herring salads, Salmon	**Rosé**
Poultry (roasted), Snails	Light red wine **Vin rouge léger** (i.e. Beaujolais)
Beef (steak), Mutton (roasted or grilled)	Red wine **Vin rouge** (i.e. Côtes du Rhône, Châteauneuf-du-Pape)
Game	Full-bodied red wine **Vin rouge corsé** (i.e. Bourgogne, Médoc, St. Emilion)

salē	salut	*hi*
sä vä	ça va?	*how are you?*
mäläd	malade	*sick*
tāt	la tête	*head*
zhā māl älätät	j'ai mal à la tête	*I have a headache*
väNt(ər)	le ventre	*stomach*
zhā māl ō väNt(ər)	j'ai mal au ventre	*I have a stomach-ache*
fē•āv(ər)	la fièvre	*fever*
ēsē	ici	*here*
färmäsē	la pharmacie	*pharmacy*
kôNprēmā	le comprimé	*tablet*
ēl mə fō dā kôNprēmā	il me faut des comprimés	*I need some tablets*

In case of emergency

There is a list of doctors and pharmacies in the local phone book.
You can also ask at the hotel, local police station (**gendarmerie**) or
check the local newspapers for the doctor or pharmacy on duty (**de garde**), especially during weekends and at night.

14 Sick

PHARMACIE

_'__ ___ _ __ ____.
I have a headache.

_'__ ___ __ _____.
I have a stomach-ache.
___.
Here.

_'__ __ __ _____.
I have a fever.

__ _____
I would like
___ _____.
some tablets.

→
3 Pharmacy
5 Fever

↓ 1 Sick
2 Tablet
4 Here

73

täksē	**le taxi**	*taxi*
äplā eN täksē	**appelez un taxi**	*call a taxi*
eN mômäN	**un moment**	*just a moment*
älägär	**à la gare**	*to the train station*
älä•ärōpôr	**à l'aéroport**	*to the airport*
älôtel fräNs	**à l'Hôtel FRANCE**	*to the FRANCE hotel*
rē	**rue**	*street*
ärätā vōō	**arrêtez-vous**	*stop*

Taxis

French taxis come in all different shapes and colors! There is no standard yellow or black cab but you will recognize them by the sign on the roof. When the sign is lighted, this means the taxi is available. Always make sure that the meter is running.

Taxi stand

15 Taxi

Answers

Lesson 1

D'où part le vol 105?
Porte numéro deux,
monsieur.

Je voudrais enregistrer
mes bagages.

Très bien.

Votre carte d'embarquement,
s'il vous plaît.

Merci. Bon voyage!

Lesson 2

Je voudrais louer une voiture.

Super ou ordinaire?

Super.

Le plein?
Oui, s'il vous plaît.

Votre ticket, s'il vous plaît.
Trente francs.

Paris, Fontainebleau, Beaune,
Châlons, Lyon, Avignon, Nice

Lesson 3

Bonsoir.
Bonsoir, monsieur.

Une chambre, s'il vous plaît.
Oui.
Une chambre à deux lits.

Pour combien de jours?
Pour cinq jours.

C'est combien, la chambre?
Trois cents francs.
Très bien.

3 OUI   1 BIEN
5 BONSOIR   2 JOUR
6 CHAMBRE   4 COMBIEN
7 LIT
8 MONSIEUR

Lesson 4

Le petit déjeuner, c'est où?
À droite, madame.

Bonjour, madame. Café? Thé?
Café au lait, s'il vous plaît.

Voilà le café, les croissants,
la confiture et le beurre.

Vous désirez un jus d'orange?
Oui!

1 BONJOUR	CONFITURE
2 BEURRE	ORANGE
3 JUS	CROISSANT
4 CAFÉ	

Lesson 5

Un plan de Paris, s'il vous plaît.
Voilà, madame.
Merci beaucoup.

Où est le Louvre?
Station de métro Palais-Royal.

Le métro est à gauche.

Le métro va à Palais-Royal?
Oui.

Pardon, où est le Louvre?
Je ne sais pas.

Tout droit, madame.
Merci, monsieur.

Un billet, s'il vous plaît.

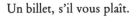

3 BEAUCOUP	1 LOUVRE
5 MÉTRO	2 PARDON
7 OUI	4 OÙ
10 PLAN	6 BILLET
11 MERCI	8 PARIS
12 STATION	9 MUSÉE

Lesson 6

Un café au lait, s'il vous plaît.

Il fait chaud.

Vous êtes Américain?
Oui, je suis de New York.

Les États-Unis sont beaux.
La France aussi.

J'aime la France.

Une cigarette?
Merci beaucoup, monsieur.

Lesson 7

C'est combien, les lunettes de soleil?
Cent francs.

Bien.

Et avec cela?
Merci, c'est tout.

Où est le bureau de change?
Le bureau de change?
La Société-Générale est là-bas.

Bonjour, monsieur.
Je veux changer deux cents dollars.
Votre passeport, s'il vous plaît.
Voilà mille francs.

Merci, monsieur. Au revoir.

4 TOUT	1 CHANGER
5 PASSEPORT	2 BUREAU
7 MONSIEUR	3 CENT
8 LÀ	6 SOLEIL
9 MERCI	
10 MILLE	
11 LUNETTES (DE SOLEIL)	
12 FRANC	

Lesson 8

Ces cartes postales, s'il vous plaît.
Cinq francs.

Vous avez des timbres?
Non, madame, la poste est là-bas.

C'est combien, une carte postale
pour les États-Unis?

Deux francs quarante.

Cinq timbres, s'il vous plaît.

1 FRANC
2 TIMBRE
3 POSTE
4 CARTE

Lesson 9

Une glace, s'il vous plaît.
Vanille? Chocolat? Fraise?

Vanille, s'il vous plaît.

Un pédalo.
C'est combien par heure?
Vingt francs.

C'est très cher.

Je voudrais un parasol.
C'est combien?
Cent francs.

Bien.

Et avec cela?
Une huile solaire.

3 CHOCOLAT	1 GLACE
5 CHER	2 PARASOL
7 FRAISES	3 HEURE
8 VANILLE	6 BIEN

Lesson 10

Vous désirez, madame?
Cinq oranges.

Et avec cela?
Un kilo de tomates, s'il vous plaît.

Les bananes sont excellentes.
Non, merci.

Regardez l'ail.
Non, non!

Si!
L'ail est très bon
dans la salade de tomates.

1 BANANE
2 SALADE
3 ORANGE
4 TOMATE

Lesson 11

Allô.

Je veux réserver une table
pour deux personnes pour demain soir.

Bien. Votre nom, s'il vous plaît.

Mon nom est Smith.

Smith?

Oui. Quand est le spectacle?

Le dîner est à huit heures,
madame.

2 RÉSERVER
3 NOM
4 TABLE
5 SOIR
6 PERSONNE

1 DEMAIN

Lesson 12

Bonsoir.
Une table pour deux personnes.

Vous désirez?
Viande, poisson, poulet rôti,
omelette?

Deux poulets rôtis, s'il vous plaît.

Une soupe? Une soupe à l'oignon?
Un potage à la tomate?

Deux soupes à l'oignon.
C'est tout?
Oui.

Voilà deux poulets rôtis.
Bon appétit.

Vous avez terminé?
Oui.

L'addition, s'il vous plaît.

3 SOUPE	1 POULET
4 OMELETTE	2 APPÉTIT
6 ADDITION	5 TOMATE
8 RÔTI	7 POISSON
10 VIANDE	9 TABLE

Lesson 13

Bonjour, vous désirez?
Un café crème.
Un cognac.
Un jus d'orange.

Une bière, s'il vous plaît.
Un vin rouge.
Le vin rouge français est excellent.

Lesson 14

Salut!
Salut, Sandrine!

Ça va?
Je suis malade. J'ai mal à la tête.

Où est la pharmacie?

J'ai mal à la tête.
J'ai mal au ventre. Ici.
J'ai de la fièvre.
Je voudrais des comprimés.

3 PHARMACIE
5 FIÈVRE
7 TÊTE

1 MALADE
2 COMPRIMÉ
4 ICI
6 VENTRE

Lesson 15

Appelez un taxi, s'il vous plaît.
Oui, monsieur, un moment.

Où?
À la gare, s'il vous plaît.

Arrêtez-vous ici.

C'est combien?
Cent francs.

Word-Building Puzzle

Puzzle on page 90

Let's go to a famous cabaret tonight:
MOULIN ROUGE

Major French sports event:
TOUR DE FRANCE

Structure in the south of France:
PONT D'AVIGNON

Food & Drink

Puzzle on page 104

AIL	OIGNON
JUS	ORANGE
THÉ	POULET
VIN	SALADE
CAFÉ	TOMATE
BIÈRE	VIANDE
FRUIT	POISSON
GLACE	VANILLE
SOUPE	CHOCOLAT
BANANE	OMELETTE
BEURRE	CONFITURE
COGNAC	CROISSANT
FRAISE	

Syllable Puzzle

Puzzle on pages 110/111

1. TAXI
2. SOLEIL
3. ESSENCE
4. FRANC
5. LUNETTES
6. PARASOL
7. COGNAC
8. BANANE
9. ORANGE
10. FRAISE
11. VIN
12. TIMBRE
13. CROISSANT
14. POULET
15. TOMATE
16. POISSON
17. LIT
18. TABLE
19. BILLET
20. PÉDALO
21. MÉTRO
22. FROMAGE

Reader Information:

You have already learned about 200 words and phrases. Approximately 800 more commonly used words follow. Choose from these words as you please to build up your own vocabulary, according to your needs. Phonetic transcriptions have not been given here but with the knowledge you have gained from the chapters you will be able to manage.

Mini-Dictionary for Tourists

English-French

Find the appropriate French word as needed.

a/an	un, une	*au gratin*	gratin
accelerator	accélérateur	*August*	août
accident	accident	*Australia*	Australie
address	adresse	*Australian*	australien
afternoon	après-midi		
air-filter	filtre à air		
airport	aéroport	*bad*	mauvais
almonds	amandes	*bag*	sac
alternate route	itinéraire-bis	*bakery*	boulangerie, pâtisserie
America	Amérique	*banana*	banane
American	américain	*band-aid*	tricostéril
ambulance	ambulance	*bandage*	pansement
and	et	*bank*	banque
anticyclone	anticyclone	*bar*	bar, brasserie
apple sauce	compote de pommes	*bathroom*	salle de bains, toilettes
area code	indicatif	*battery*	pile, batterie
as far as	jusqu'à	*beach*	plage
asparagus	asperge	*beach umbrella*	parasol
assorted	assorti, varié		

B

89

Word-Building Puzzle

(Answers on page 87)

Write the letters of the French words in the boxes as indicated. For example, if the number "2" appears, write the second letter of the word suggested by the picture.

Let's go to a famous cabaret tonight:

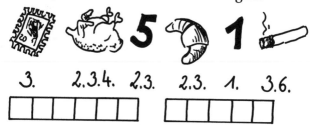

3.   2.3.4.   2.3.   2.3.   1.   3.6.

☐☐☐☐☐   ☐☐☐☐☐

Major French sports event:

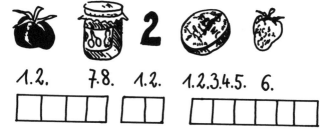

1.2.   7.8.   1.2.   1.2.3.4.5.   6.

☐☐☐☐   ☐☐   ☐☐☐☐☐☐

Structure in the south of France:

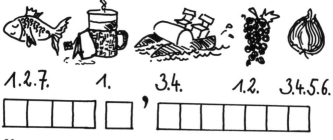

1.2.7.   1.   3.4.   1.2.   3.4.5.6.

☐☐☐☐☐   ☐ ' ☐☐☐☐☐☐

beans	haricots	bridge	pont
beautiful	beau	Britain	Grande Bretagne
bed	lit	British	britannique
bedroom	chambre	broth	bouillon
beef	bœuf	brown	marron
beefsteak	bifteck	bulb	ampoule
beer	bière	bumper	pare-chocs
beer on tap	bière à la pression	bun	brioche
belt	ceinture, courroie	bus	bus, autobus, autocar
bicycle	bicyclette, vélo	bus stop	arrêt de bus, d'autobus
bikini	bikini	business hours	heures d'ouverture
bill	facture, note (hôtel)	butcher's shop	boucherie
bitter	amer	butter	beurre
black	noir	buy	acheter
black currant	cassis		
blue	bleu		

C

boar	sanglier	cabbage	chou
board	plateau, tableau	cafe	café, brasserie
		cake	gâteau, pâtisserie
boarding school, house	pension	camera	appareil-photo
		camping ground	terrain de camping
boat	bateau, barque	Canada	Canada
boiled	bouilli	Canadian	canadien
boiled egg	œuf à la coque	candy	bonbons
booth	cabine	car	voiture
border	frontière	car rental	location de voitures
bottle	bouteille		
bottle opener	ouvre-bouteille	carbon dioxide	gaz carbonique
brakes	freins	carburetor	carburateur
brandy	cognac	carrot	carotte
bread	pain	cash register	caisse
breakfast	petit déjeuner	cashier	caissier
breakdown	panne		

Soupe à l'oignon   *Onion soup*

1-1/2 pounds (680 g) large onions 6 tablespoons (90 ml) unsalted butter	Cut onions into thin slices, crosswise and sauté in butter in large soup pot until browned, not burned.

6 cups (1-1/2 L) beef broth	Add broth salt, pepper, bouquet garni and cognac. Stir and bring to a boil.
Salt & black pepper to taste Bouquet garni 1 tablespoon cognac	Turn down heat and let simmer for 20 minutes.

1/2 cup (55 g) grated gruyère cheese	Remove bouquet garni. Stir in grated cheese, reserving some for the top.
Thick slices French bread	Preheat oven to 425° (220° C). Pour soup into an ovenproof tureen and top with bread slices and remaining grated cheese.
	Bake for 15 minutes, or until cheese browns and becomes bubbly.

Serve hot with some freshly ground pepper and a chilled glass of white wine.

castle	château	clothes for men	vêtements pour hommes
cathedral	cathédrale		
cauliflower	chou-fleur	cloudy	nuageux
celery	céleri	clutch	embrayage
cent	centime	cock	coq
centimeter	centimètre	coffee with milk	café au lait
chair	chaise		
champagne	champagne	coffee house	café
change	changer, monnaie	collision	collision
		color	couleur
charge	mettre sur un compte, recharger une batterie	color-film	film en couleurs, pellicule couleur
check	addition, chèque. contrôler, enregistrer	conserve (of goose)	confit (d'oie)
		consommé	consommé
		consulate	consulat
cheese	fromage	cookies	biscuits, petits fours
cheese platter	plateau de fromages		
cherry	cerise	cool	frais
cherry pie	clafoutis	cork	bouchon
chic	chic	cork screw	tire-bouchon
chicken	poulet	corn	maïs
chocolate	chocolat	course	plat
choice	choix	crab	crabe
church	église	cream	crème
cigar	cigare	credit card	carte de crédit
cigarette, pack of cigarettes	cigarette, paquet de cigarettes		
		croissant	croissant
		cup	tasse
city	ville	curve	virage
city tour	tour de la ville	customs	douane
		cutlet	côtelette
closed	fermé		
cloth	tissu	danger	danger
wash cloth	gant de toilette	day	jour
		dead	mort, à plat

D

Gratin Dauphinois   *Potatoes au gratin*

4 cups (1 L) milk	Boil milk and let cool.
2 eggs	Beat eggs and stir into cooled milk. Set aside.
2 pounds (1 kg) potatoes	Peel potatoes and pat dry. Cut into thin slices.
1 clove garlic, cut in half	Rub garlic inside a large ovenproof gratin dish and then butter it well.
4 ounces (115 g) unsalted butter cut into small pieces	Make a layer of potatoes and sprinkle with salt, pepper, and nutmeg.
Salt, pepper, nutmeg	Repeat this procedure until dish is 3/4 full.
1/2 pound (250 g) gruyère cheese, grated	Sprinkle with grated cheese and dot with pieces of butter.
4 ounces (115 g) unsalted butter, cut into small pieces	Pour milk/egg mixture over potatoes until just covered.
	Preheat oven to 375° (190° C) Bake for about 45 minutes. The gratin should become thick and the top should form a golden crust.

This is a classic family recipe and is delicious served with meats, poultry and game. Served generously, it can even be enjoyed as a meal in itself.

dead end	impasse	emergency exit	sortie de secours
dear	cher, coûteux	England	Angleterre
decaffeinated	décaféiné	English	anglais
deck	pont	entrance	entrée
deep	grave	eurocheque	eurochèque
deer	chevreuil	exchange	changer
degree	degré	excellent	excellent
delay	retard	excuse me	pardon
dentist	dentiste	exit	sortie
department store	grand magasin	express subway	R.E.R. (Réseau Express Régional- à Paris)
dessert	dessert		
detour	déviation		
direction	direction		
dish	assiette		
distance	distance		
door	porte	far	loin
double room	chambre à deux lits	fast	rapide, vite
		fast train	express
doughnut	beignet	fender	garde-boue
downtown	centre ville	fever	fièvre
dress	robe	filet	filet
drink	boisson	film	film, pellicule
driver's license	permis de conduire	filter	filtre
		fire extinguisher	extincteur
duck	canard		
		first aid	secours
		first aid kit	trousse de secours, boîte de pharmacie
E east	est		
eat	manger		
eau de cologne	eau de cologne	first floor	rez-de-chaussée
egg	œuf		
electric razor	rasoir électrique	first name	prénom
		fish	poisson
elegant	élégant	fish soup	bouillabaisse
elevator	ascenseur	flash	flash
embassy	ambassade	flat tire	pneu crevé

F

Poule au Pot	*Chicken with vegetables*
1 good size chicken	Put chicken in a large pot and cover with cold water. Bring to a boil, skim and reduce to simmer.
Salt & black pepper, bay leaf, thyme *2 cloves garlic, minced*	Add salt, bay leaf, thyme and garlic. Cook for about 1 hour. Chicken should be tender, not mushy.
3-4 carrots *3-4 turnips* *1/4 pound (115 g) small onions* *4-5 leeks* *4-5 celery stalks*	Wash and peel vegetables then cut into large pieces. Use only white parts of leeks. Cut off celery leaves, use stalks. Vegetables should be added as follows: carrots + turnips 40 minutes before chicken is cooked; onions, 20 minutes before; leeks + celery, 10 minutes before. Take out cooked hen and vegetables and place in separate dishes. Remove bay leaf. Keep warm in oven until ready to serve.

This is an all-time classic. King Henri IV wanted "une poule au pot" for everyone on Sundays. This recipe had been forgotten for a while but has recently enjoyed renewed success.
Serve with rice and a nice bottle of wine.

flight	vol
floor	étage
flyer	prospectus
fog	brouillard
food	aliments
forbidden	interdit
foreign exchange office	bureau de change
fork	fourchette
form	formulaire
France	France
franc	franc
free	gratuit, libre
French	français
French franc	franc français
french fries	frites
fresh	frais
Friday	vendredi
frog	grenouille
frogs' legs	cuisses de grenouille
fruit	fruits
fuel	gasoil, gazole
full	plein
full board	pension complète
fuse	fusible

G

game	gibier
garage	garage
garden	jardin
garlic	ail
gas	essence
gas station	station service
glass	verre
glasses	lunettes

glove	gant
go	aller
go by	passer
good	bon, bien
good bye	au revoir
good evening	bonsoir
good morning	bonjour
goose liver	foie gras d'oie
gourmet	gourmet
gram	gramme
grape	raisin
grapefruit	pamplemousse
gravel	gravillons
green	vert
grey	gris
grilled	grillé
meats, etc.	grillade
guarantee of origin and of production method	appellation contrôlée (pour les vins, fromages, etc.)
guide	guide
guilty	coupable

H

hairdresser	coiffeur
half-board	demi-pension
half-hour	demi-heure
ham	jambon
hammer	marteau
handkerchief	mouchoir
harbor	port
hare	lièvre
hat	chapeau
head	tête
headache	mal de tête
heart	cœur

Pommes Cuites au Four   *Baked apples*

4 tablespoons (60 ml) unsalted butter	Cream together butter and sugar in a bowl.
6 tablespoons (90 ml) sugar	Fill apple centers with mixture.
6 apples, peeled and cored	

2 pounds (1 kg) pastry (*you can use ready-made pie crust*)	Roll out dough and cut into 6 squares, large enough to wrap the apples.
1 egg, beaten	Center apples in dough squares and cover apples entirely. Pinch top of dough to form an apple stem. Brush with beaten egg.
	Preheat oven to 350° (175° C). Place apple in an oven-proof dish and bake for 30 minutes.

This old-fashioned recipe is found in various regions of France under different names: Pommes en cage (Savoie), Bourdelots, (Normandie), Rabotes, Douillons, etc . . .
This simple dessert—an apple in a pastry case—has always been very popular.

heart attack	crise cardiaque
hello	bonjour, allô (téléphone)
help	secours
hen	poule
herbal tea	infusion, tisane
here	ici
here is	voici
hi	bonjour, salut
highway	autoroute
home fries	pommes de terre sautées
honey	miel
hospital	hôpital
hotel	hôtel
hour	heure
house	maison
how much	combien
hunter	chasseur
husband	mari

I

I	je, moi
ice	glace, verglas (sur la route)
ice cream	glace, crème glacée
island	île
indigestion	indigestion
information	renseignements, in-formation

insurance	assurance
Ireland	Irlande
Irish	irlandais

J

jack	cric
jacket (suit)	veste
jam	confiture
juice	jus
July	juillet
June	juin

K

key	clé
kilogram	kilo(gramme)
knife	couteau
know	savoir

L

lady	dame
lager	bière blonde
lake	lac
lamb (leg of)	gigot
lard	lard
lawyer	avocat
lean	maigre
left	gauche
left luggage	consigne
lemon	citron
lentils	lentilles
letter	lettre
lettuce	laitue
license plate	plaque d' immatricu-lation
lighter	briquet
liqueur	liqueur, digestif
little (a)	peu, un peu
lobster	homard
local train	train de banlieue

Crêpes

French pancakes

2-1/2 cups (250 g) all-purpose flour 1/2 cup (120 g) sugar Pinch of salt	In a bowl, mix dry ingredients together.
3 eggs	Add eggs, 1 at a time, mix well.
4 tablespoons (60 ml) unsalted butter, melted 1 teaspoon (5 ml) vanilla 2 tablespoons (30 ml) Cognac	Add melted butter, vanilla and Cognac.
1-1/2 cups (12 fluid ounces) milk	Stir in milk little by little. Batter should be creamy.
Butter for cooking	Let batter sit for at least one hour. Cook crêpes in a small hot frying pan brushed with butter for about 1 minute per side.

You can eat crêpes plain or with sugar, jam, honey, etc. for dessert. Or for a main meal, they can be accompanied by eggs, ham, meats, sauces: any kind of filling you may think of. Crêpes are especially popular in Brittany (Crêpes bretonnes) and there are as many varieties of crêpes in France as of bread!

lockers (*luggage*)	consigne automatique	*moped*	cyclomoteur
love	aimer	*morning*	matin
luggage	bagage	*motel*	motel
lunch	déjeuner	*mountain*	montagne
		mountaineer-ing	alpinisme
mackerel	maquereau		
madam, Mrs.	madame	*movie theater*	cinéma
magazine	revue, magazine	*Mrs., madam*	madame
		Mr., sir	monsieur
maid	femme de ménage	*much*	beaucoup
		museum	musée
mail box	boîte aux lettres	*mushroom* (*cultivated*)	champignon (de Paris)
map (*of the city*)	plan (de la ville)	*mussel*	moule
		mustard	moutarde
mashed potatoes	purée de pommes de terre	*my*	ma, mon
match	allumettes	*name*	nom
maximum speed	vitesse maximale	*napkin*	serviette
		narrow	étroit
meal	repas	*nationality*	nationalité
meat	viande	*nature*	nature
medical emergency	S.O.S. médecins	*newspaper*	journal
		night	nuit
Mediterra-nean sea	mer méditer-ranée	*no*	non
		noodles	nouilles
menu	menu	*north*	nord
meter	mètre	*notebook*	carnet
midday	midi	*nudism*	nudisme
mileage	kilométrage	*number*	numéro
mineral water	eau minérale		
mint	menthe	*oil*	huile
minute	minute	*oil level*	niveau d' huile
Miss	mademoiselle	*oil change*	vidange
Monday	lundi	*omelette*	omelette
moment	moment	*one-way*	sens unique
money	argent	*onion*	oignon
		onion soup	soupe à l'oignon

N

O

CAMEMBERT
fabriqué en Normandie
Plaisir DE FRANCE

Fett i.Tr.
GRASO
45 %
POUR CENT
DE MATIÈRE GRASSE

POIDS NET A L'EMBALLAGE
NETTO GEWICHT
NET WEIGHT
PESO NETO
℮ INH 250g

FULL FAT SOFT CHEESE

3 161911 395351

Enjoying cheese:

At the end of lunch and dinner, the waiter will present you a platter of different types of cheese. You should choose 2-3 different kinds and then the waiter will cut them for you.

The various cheeses are cut as follows:

. . . the round or square soft cheese is cut like a cake,

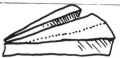

. . . the small goat's milk cheese is cut in half,
. . . the piece of Brie is cut into long triangles,

. . . the tall cylindrical cheese is cut into thin sheets,
. . . the hard cheese is cut lying down into slanted slices.

open	ouvert	*policeman*	agent de police
or	ou	*pork*	porc
order	commander	*postcard*	carte postale
oyster	huitre	*post office*	bureau de poste
paddle boat	pédalo	*potato*	pomme de terre
pancake	crêpe	*pot roast*	pot-au-feu
pants	pantalon	*pressure cooker*	cocotte-minute
pardon	pardon	*pretty*	joli
parking	stationne-ment, parking	*price*	prix
		primary road	route nationale
parsley	persil	*pumpkin*	citrouille
pass by	passer		
passport	passeport	*quarter of an hour*	quart d'heure **Q**
pâté	pâté		
pay	payer	*rabbit*	lapin **R**
pay (t.v.)	payant (télé payante)	*radiator*	radiateur
peach	pêche	*railway*	chemin de fer
pear	poire	*rain*	pluie
peas	pois	*raspberry*	framboise
pepper	poivre	*raw*	cru
perfume	parfum	*raw vegetables*	crudités
photo (graph)	photo (graphie)	*receiver*	récepteur
pie (apple)	tarte (aux pommes)	*red*	rouge
		red currant	groseille
pigeon	pigeon	*registration*	carte grise
pike	brochet	*reminder*	rappel
pilgrimage	pèlerinage	*rent*	louer
plane	avion	*reservation*	réservation
plate	assiette	*reserve*	réserver
platform	quai	*rest area*	aire de repos
please	s'il vous plaît	*restroom*	toilettes
plum	prune	*restaurant*	restaurant
police	police, gen-darmerie	*rice*	riz

103

Food & Drink

(Answers on page 87)

25 French words related to food and drink appear in the diagram. They can be found horizontally or vertically. The 25 words are:

```
JUSCOGNACFF
COIGNONAORR
RTHEUMVINUA
ORANGEGLFII
IVANILLEITS
SALADEAPTPE
SOUPETCOUOB
ATOMATEURIE
NBIEREULESU
TOVIANDEUSR
CHOCOLATROR
CAFEVBANANE
```

right	droite	see	regarder
right of way	priorité	self-service	libre service
rinse	rincer	service	service
ripe	mûr	included	compris
river	rivière	shade, shadow	ombre
road	route, voie	shampoo	shampooing
road map	carte routière	sheep	mouton
road work	travaux	sherbet	sorbet
roast	rôti	shellfish	coquillage
rolls	petits pains	shift	changement
room number	numéro de		de vitesse
	chambre	shish-kebab	brochette
rosé	rosé	ship	bateau
		shirt	chemise
saddle (of	selle (de	shock	amortisseurs
mutton)	mouton)	absorbers	
safety belt	ceinture de	shoe	chaussure
	securité	shoes	paire de
sail boat	voilier		chaussures
salad	salade	short	court
salt	sel	shower (rain)	averse
salted	salé	shower	douche
sandwich	sandwich	shrimp	crevette
sanitary	serviette	sir, Mr.	monsieur
napkin	hygiénique	size	pointure
Saturday	samedi	skirt	jupe
sauce	sauce	sky	ciel
sauerkraut	choucroute	sleeping car	couchette
sausage	saucisse	sleeping pills	somnifère
sautéed	sauté	small change	monnaie
scarf	foulard	smoked	fumé
schedule	horaire	snack	casse-croûte
Scotland	Écosse	snail	escargot
Scottish	écossais	snow	neige
screwdriver	tournevis	soap	savon
sea	mer	sock	socquette
seafood	fruits de mer	soft	doux
seasoning	assaisonne-	sole	sole
	ment	soufflé	soufflé

soup	soupe	store	magasin
south	sud	straight ahead	tout droit
spare part	pièce de rechange	strawberry	fraise
		stuffed	farci
spare tire	roue de secours	subway	métro
		subway station	station de métro
spark plug	bougie		
spinach	épinards	sugar	sucre
spoon	cuiller	suitcase	valise
square	place	sun	soleil
stairs	escaliers	sunburn	coup de soleil
stamp	timbre	sunglasses	lunettes de soleil
starter	démarreur		
station	gare	suntan oil	huile solaire
stay	séjour	Sunday	dimanche
steak	steak	sunny spell	éclaircie
steakhouse	rôtisserie, grill	super	super
steering wheel	volant	supermarket	supermarché
stockings	bas, collant	surf board	planche à voile
stomach	ventre	sweater	pull-over
stop (bus)	station	sweet	sucré, doux

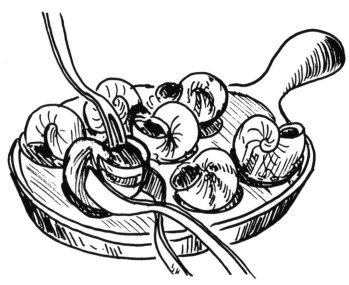

swim	nager	tongue	langue
swimming pool	piscine	tooth brush	brosse à dents
		tooth paste	dentifrice
		tourist	touriste
table	table	tourist office	syndicat d'initiative
tan	bronzer		
tasting	dégustation	tow truck	service de dépannage
taxi	taxi		
taxi stand	station de taxi	tower	tour
tea	thé	town	ville
tea room	salon de thé	traffic jam	embouteillage
telegram	télégramme	train	train
telephone	téléphone	trip	voyage, excursion
telephone booth	cabine télé-phonique		
		trout	truite
temperature	température	truck	camion, poids lourd
tender	tendre		
tennis	tennis	trunk	coffre
tennis court	court de tennis	Tuesday	mardi
terrace	terrasse	umbrella	parapluie **U**
thank you	merci	unlimited	illimité
theater	théâtre	unleaded	essence sans plomb
there	là		
over there	là-bas	use	utiliser, consommer
thirst	soif		
thunderstorm	orage		
Thursday	jeudi	valuables	objets de valeur **V**
ticket	billet, contraven-tion		
		vanilla	vanille
		veal	veau
tip	pourboire	veal cutlet	escalope de veau
tire	pneu		
tire pressure	pression des pneus	vegetables	légumes
		visit	visite
today	aujourd'hui		
toll	péage	waiter	garçon, serveur **W**
tomato	tomate		
tomorrow	demain	wake up	réveiller

Numbers

0	zéro	32	trente-deux
1	un	40	quarante
2	deux	50	cinquante
3	trois	60	soixante
4	quatre	70	soixante-dix (= 60 + 10)
5	cinq	71	soixante et onze
6	six	72	soixante-douze
7	sept	73	soixante-treize . . .
8	huit	80	quatre-vingts (= 4 × 20)
9	neuf	81	quatre-vingt-un
10	dix	82	quatre-vingt-deux
11	onze	90	quatre-vingt-dix
12	douze	99	quatre-vingt-dix-neuf
13	treize	100	cent
14	quatorze	200	deux cents
15	quinze	201	deux cent un
16	seize	210	deux cent dix
17	dix-sept	400	quatre cents
18	dix-huit	500	cinq cents
19	dix-neuf	1,000	mille
20	vingt	2,000	deux mille
21	vingt et un	2,010	deux mille dix
22	vingt deux	3,000	trois mille
23	vingt-trois . . .	10,000	dix mille
30	trente	100,000	cent mille
31	trente et un	1,000,000	un million

Wales	Pays de Galles
walk	se promener
walnut	noix
want	vouloir
warm	chaud
watch	surveiller
watch	montre
water	eau
water-skiing	ski nautique
weather	temps
wear out	user
Wednesday	mercredi
week	semaine
welsh	gallois
well-done	bien cuit
west	ouest
wheel	roue
when	quand
where	où
wife	femme
whipped cream	crème chantilly
white	blanc
white bread	pain blanc
white wine	vin blanc

wind	vent
windshield	pare-brise
wine	vin
wire	fil de fer
wish	désirer
with	avec
witness	témoin
woman	femme
women's clothes	vêtements pour femme
work (does not)	(ne) marche (pas)
wounded	blessé

Y

yellow	jaune
yes	oui
yesterday	hier
yogurt	yogourt
you	vous
your	votre
youth hostel	auberge de jeunesse

Z

zero	zéro
zip code	code postal

Syllable Puzzle

(Answers on page 87)

Form 19 words from these syllables and write them down. Picture clues and the number of syllables in each word are given on the next page.

BA	BIL	BLE	BRE	CE	CO	CROIS	DA
ES	FRAI	FRANC	FRO	GE	GE	GNAC	LEIL
LET	LET					LIT	LO
LU	ME					MA	MA
NA	NE					NET	O
PA	PE					POIS	POU
RA	RAN	SANT	SE	SEN	SO	SOL	SON
TA	TA	TE	TES	TIM	TO	TRO	XI
							VIN

111

Useful Addresses:

American Embassy
2, Rue Gabriel
75008   PARIS
42.96.12.02

British Embassy
35, Rue du Faubourg St. Honoré
75383   PARIS Cédex 08
42.66.91.42

American Consulate-General
72, Rue Général-Sarrail
69006 LYON
78.24.68.49

British Consulate-General
16, Rue d'Anjou
75008 PARIS
42.66.91.42

Canadian Embassy
35, Avenue Montaigne
75008   PARIS
47.23.01.01

Australian Embassy
4, Rue Jean-Rey
75015   PARIS
45.75.62.00

Canadian Consulate-General
Edifice Bonnel, Par-Dieu
coin Bonnel et Garibaldy
Rue de Bonnel, 3e étage
69003 LYON
72.61.15.25

au Marche De Provence